Tiny Talks

Volume 4
The Family

A year's worth of simple messages that can be given during Primary or Family Home Evening

Tiny Talks

Volume 4
The Family

A year's worth of simple messages that can be given during Primary or Family Home Evening

By Tammy & Chad Daybell

Illustrated by Rhett E. Murray

CFI

Springville, Utah

ISBN: 1-55517-721-2
e.1

Published by CFI
Imprint of Cedar Fort Inc.
www.cedarfort.com

Distributed by:

Cover design © 2004 by Lyle Mortimer
Illustrations © 2003 by Rhett E. Murray

Printed in the United States of America
10 9 8 7 6 5 4 3 2 1

Printed on acid-free paper

Table of Contents

Introduction

As parents, we have experienced the challenge of writing Primary talks that are simple enough for our children to read, but that are interesting to the children in the audience. To help other parents in our situation, we have created the *Tiny Talks* series.

Volume 1 is linked to the 2002 Primary theme of *Temples* and their importance. The theme of Volume 2 is *The Savior*. It was written to help Primary children understand the mission of Jesus Christ and grow closer to him. Volume 3 focuses on the 2003 Primary theme of *The Church of Jesus Christ* and the restored gospel.

This fourth volume is tied to the 2004 Primary theme "*My Family Can Be Forever*." Many stories in this volume come from the childhood experiences of the modern prophets. We have purposely focused on stories involving the more recent prophets.

These stories are entertaining and often include a hint of humor, but more importantly, they show what it means to be a young member of the Church of Jesus Christ of Latter-day Saints.

Hopefully the children of the Church will gain greater appreciation for these great men who have served as our prophets.

These talks can be used in many settings, including Family Home Evening. If a talk is used in Primary, we suggest the child give the talk while holding up the picture at the appropriate time. The child could conclude with a short testimony about the topic, and close by saying, "In the name of Jesus Christ, amen."

At the end of some of the talks you will find small footnote numbers. These correspond to the list of sources at the back of the book.

We have found that visual aids greatly enhance a talk. With each talk we have listed pictures that could be used from the Gospel Art Picture Kit (GAPK). It is available from the Church Distribution Center. If you don't have one, your meetinghouse library might have a set. The meetinghouse library may also have other pictures available that fit the talk.

Thank you for your support of this series.

Tammy and Chad Daybell

Chapter 1:

I am a child of God

We are all children of heavenly parents

We are all part of a family. No matter what happens to us here on earth, we need to always remember that we are the spirit children of heavenly parents. We are created in their image, meaning we look like they do.

We are part of a big eternal family that lived together in heaven before we were born. Everyone on earth is our spirit brother or sister. While we were in heaven we learned about the gospel. Heavenly Father told us about a plan that would help us become like him.

We knew that our heavenly parents had resurrected bodies. In order for us to receive such a body, we would first have to go to earth and receive a mortal body. That is part of the eternal plan. Our heavenly parents want all of us to return and live with them in heaven.

That is why we are each sent to earth and become part of a family. Our purpose in life is to keep the commandments, live good lives, and help each other make it back to live with our heavenly parents again. If we do our very best here on earth, we can live together forever with our family.

We followed Heavenly Father's plan

Before we were born, we were invited to attend a very special meeting called the Council in Heaven. Heavenly Father held this meeting with all of his spirit children. He told us about a wonderful plan that would allow us to go to earth and receive mortal bodies. While we were on earth, we would be tested to see if we would obey Heavenly Father's commandments. If we were righteous, we would return to live in heaven forever.

Heavenly Father told us that one of our spirit brothers, Jesus Christ, would be our Savior. Jesus would make it possible for us to repent of our sins and live in heaven again. We loved Jesus and we knew he would fulfill Heavenly Father's plan.

But some of the spirit children didn't like the plan. Their leader was Satan. He wanted to make his own rules and not follow Heavenly Father's plan. This was wrong, and Satan and those that followed him were cast out of heaven. We were sad that they were disobedient, but we knew that Heavenly Father's plan is the only way for us to be happy and to live forever with our families.

Scripture

And he called upon our father Adam by his own voice, saying: I am God; I made the world, and men before they were in the flesh.
(Moses 6:51)

Visual Aid:
GAPK # 608
Christ and Children From Around the World

Adam and Eve were sent to earth

Scripture:

So God created man in his own image, in the image of God created he him; male and female created he them.
(Genesis 1:27)

After we accepted Heavenly Father's plan, we watched the creation of the earth as it was prepared for us. We watched the land be created, and saw the sun and moon in the sky. Then Heavenly Father placed many kinds of animals on the earth. Finally, Adam and Eve were placed in the Garden of Eden.

We were very excited. We knew we would soon be able to come to earth and be part of a family, just as Heavenly Father had planned.

Adam and Eve were taught many things by Heavenly Father when they were in the Garden of Eden. Along with these teachings, they were told to not eat the fruit of a certain tree. If they did, they would have to leave the garden.

Satan tempted them, and they ate the fruit. Heavenly Father told them to leave the Garden of Eden and begin a family together. This was all part of the plan so we could come to earth. Jesus Christ had been chosen to be our Savior, and if we live righteously, we can return to live again with our heavenly parents.

Visual Aid:
GAPK # 101
Adam and Eve

4

Adam and Eve raised a family

After leaving the Garden of Eden, Adam and Eve began to have children and they taught their children about Heavenly Father's plan.

They soon had a son named Abel who loved Heavenly Father and obeyed the commandments. But one of his brothers, Cain, was tempted by Satan and became wicked. Cain killed his brother Abel.

This was a very sad time for Adam and Eve, but they prayed for another righteous son. Heavenly Father heard their prayers, and soon a son named Seth was born. He was a righteous man, and he looked just like his father Adam. Seth's sons and grandsons were great prophets, including great men like Enoch and Noah.

These prophets taught their families that even though we are on earth, we can always talk to Heavenly Father through prayer.

We can pray to Heavenly Father anytime and anywhere. He is always listening. It is like knocking on a door. If we knock, Heavenly Father will answer. He wants us to return and live with him again.

Scripture

Ask, and it shall be given unto you; seek, and ye shall find; knock, and it shall be opened unto you. For every one that asketh, receiveth; and he that seeketh, findeth; and to him that knocketh, it shall be opened.
(3 Nephi 14:7-8)

Visual Aid:
GAPK # 119
Adam and Eve Teaching
Their Children

5

Chapter 2:

The family is central to Heavenly Father's plan

Wilford Woodruff never forgot his parents

Scripture:

But learn that he who doeth the works of right-eousness shall receive his reward, even peace in this world, and eternal life in the world to come.
(D&C 59:23)

Visual Aid:
GAPK # 509
Wilford Woodruff

We are all part of a family. We begin life as a child, and we usually have brothers or sisters. Then as we grow older, we become a parent and a grandparent.

Wilford Woodruff knew the importance of honoring his parents, even when he was an adult. He grew up in the state of Connecticut, but after he joined the Church he moved away. He spent many years without seeing his father and stepmother. He knew they hadn't joined the Church, so he planned a special visit to see them. He wanted his family to be together forever.

Wilford returned to Connecticut and taught the gospel to his family. Wilford felt very happy when his father believed the gospel plan and asked Wilford to baptize him. Soon after, Wilford brought his parents to Salt Lake City to live with him so they could get to know their grandchildren. This was a great blessing for the whole family. Wilford told one of his daughters, "We are expecting to live together after death. I think we all as parents and children ought to make each other happy as long as we live." [1]

Lorenzo Snow knew his wife was in heaven

When Lorenzo Snow was called to be an apostle for the Church, he traveled all over the world to share the gospel. This was before telephones were invented, so the only way he could stay in touch with his family was by writing letters. So if something bad happened in the family, it would take a long time for Lorenzo to find out about it.

That's what happened when he came back to Salt Lake City after a long mission to Europe. When Lorenzo arrived home, he was told that his wife Charlotte had died a few weeks earlier. He was very sad, but he knew they had been married in the temple and that his wife had been faithful in the gospel.

A few months later, a close friend named Sister Woodward told Lorenzo a special story. She told him that Charlotte had visited her from heaven. Sister Woodward said Charlotte had been wearing white robes and looked beautiful. This made Lorenzo happy. He knew Charlotte was in heaven, and that he would live again with her someday.[2]

Scripture

And again, verily I say unto you, that whoso forbiddeth to marry is not ordained of God, for marriage is ordained of God unto man.
(D&C 49:15)

Visual Aid:
GAPK # 510
Lorenzo Snow

Brigham Young kept a lamp for each child

Scripture:

Train up a child in the way he should go: and when he is old, he will not depart from it.
(Proverbs 22:6)

Visual Aid:
GAPK # 507
Brigham Young

Brigham Young was a very busy man. He was the prophet, plus he also spent much time helping the pioneers build Salt Lake City. But he always tried to make time for his family.

Brigham felt it was important to hold family prayer each night. This way the children learned how to talk to Heavenly Father as they listened to their own father pray. But sometimes family prayer didn't go too well. Brigham's children remembered the time that one of their little sisters started running around the room and laughing loudly during the prayer. Brigham stopped the prayer, caught the little girl, took her to her mother, then returned to his spot and began praying again as if nothing had happened!

As the children got older, Brigham gave each family member their own little oil lamp. If a family member left the house after dinner, they lit their lamp and put it on the table. When people came home, they would blow out their lamp. That way, the last child home would see only one lamp lit and knew they needed to lock the door! This helped the children learn how to be responsible.[3]

A priesthood blessing saved a boy's life

When Spencer W. Kimball was six years old, a three-year-old neighbor boy named Leo Cluff was poked in the ribs by a cow's horn. It made a big gash and hurt his insides. The town doctor did the best he could for Leo, but all he could do was stitch up the injury. Before leaving, the doctor said that Leo's body was so filled with infection that he would die within a day.

But Leo's parents had faith that Leo could be healed. They called Spencer's father Andrew to come give Leo a priesthood blessing. Andrew hurried to the Cluffs' house and laid his hands on the boy's head. He blessed Leo that by the power of the priesthood he would be healed.

The next day the doctor waited in town for the Cluffs to come in and make funeral arrangements. When they did not show up, he went to the farm and was surprised to find Leo awake and healing. The doctor said, "There has been a greater power than mine at work here." Spencer was told about the blessing, and it strengthened his testimony of the power of the priesthood.[4]

Scripture

That the rights of the priesthood are inseparably connected with the powers of heaven, and that the powers of heaven cannot be controlled nor handled only upon the principles of righteousness.
(D&C 121:36)

Visual Aid:
GAPK # 517
Spencer W. Kimball

Chapter 3:

Jesus Christ makes it possible for me to live with Heavenly Father again

The Savior taught Heavenly Father's plan

Scripture:

Jesus saith unto him, I am the way, the truth, and the life: no man cometh unto the Father, but by me. (John 14:6)

Visual Aid:
GAPK # 212
Sermon on the Mount

Before we came to earth, we chose to follow Heavenly Father's plan. As part of this plan, Jesus Christ was chosen to come to earth and be our Savior. He agreed to pay the price for our sins so we can return and live with Heavenly Father again.

When Jesus came to earth, he lived near the city of Jerusalem. As he grew older, he often sat on a hillside and let the people gather around him. Then he would teach them about the gospel.

Jesus taught the people to love one another. He taught that we should forgive other people, even if they are mean to us. Jesus said if we were kind to other people, we would be blessed.

Jesus also taught that those who have the gospel should share it with other people. We should be good examples to those who aren't members of the Church.

The teachings of Jesus are found in the scriptures. The prophets have asked every family to read the scriptures together. If we follow the teachings of Jesus, we will be happy and be able to live with him again.

The Savior paid the price for our sins

Jesus Christ was sent to earth to be the Savior of the world. He taught the gospel to many people during his life, but the most important thing he did was pay the price for our sins.

The Savior's suffering began in the Garden of Gethsemane. He went to that garden to pray to Heavenly Father, and he began to feel the weight of all the the sins of the people who would ever live on earth—including yours and mine.

The Savior fell to the ground and suffered such great pain that he bled from every pore. Heavenly Father sent an angel to comfort Jesus, and he was able to complete his mission. We should always be grateful for what Jesus did for us.

What Jesus did for us is called the Atonement. That means that if we repent of our sins and do our very best to keep the commandments, we can live again with Heavenly Father and the Savior.

We should show our love for the Savior by helping our families do what is right.

Scripture

We love him, because he first loved us.
(1 John 4:19)

Visual Aid:
GAPK # 227
Jesus Praying in Gethsemane

Jesus died and then was resurrected

Scripture:

For as in Adam all die, even so in Christ shall all be made alive.
(1 Corinthians 15:22)

As members of the Church, we are very grateful for the Savior. He has made it possible for us to live with him again.

After Jesus suffered for our sins in the Garden of Gethsemane, he was taken away by wicked men. These men took Jesus to a hill near Jerusalem, where they nailed him to a cross. This hurt Jesus very much.

Jesus suffered on the cross for many hours, then he died. His body was taken by his followers and put in a tomb. But the Savior was still alive as a spirit. He went to the Spirit World and visited the great prophets who had lived before, such as Adam and Noah.

Then after three days, Jesus returned to earth. Through the power of the priesthood his body and spirit were reunited. But now the Savior's body was perfect. He would never die again.

The scriptures teach us that we will also be resurrected someday. But only those who keep the commandments will live in the Celestial Kingdom. Our goal should be to live there forever with our families.

Visual Aid:
GAPK # 234
Jesus Shows His Wounds

The Savior leads the Church today

We belong to The Church of Jesus Christ of Latter-day Saints. This is the Savior's church, and he leads it through a living prophet and the apostles.

Heavenly Father and Jesus appeared to Joseph Smith when he was fourteen years old. They told him that he would restore the true church to the earth.

The Savior gave Joseph many revelations and helped him organize the Church in the year 1830. We can read about what the Savior told Joseph to do in The Doctrine and Covenants.

When Joseph died, another prophet was chosen. His name was Brigham Young. Through him, the Savior continued to guide the Church. Ever since that time, the Savior has told his prophets how to direct the Church.

Even today, a prophet leads the Church. In 1995, the prophet gave us the Proclamation on the Family, which tells us important things about the gospel and how we should live. The prophet has told us that we should have a copy of the Proclamation in our homes. We should be grateful we have a living prophet to guide us.

Scripture

Verily, verily, I say unto you, this is my gospel; and ye know the things that ye must do in my church; for the works which ye have seen me do that shall ye also do; for that which ye have seen me do even that shall ye do; Therefore, if ye do these things blessed are ye, for ye shall be lifted up at the last day.
(3 Nephi 27:21-22)

Visual Aid:
GAPK # 240
Jesus the Christ

17

Chapter 4:

Families can be happy when they follow Jesus Christ

Heber J. Grant survived a wild sleigh ride

Scripture:

And when ye shall receive these things, I would exhort you that ye would ask God, the Eternal Father, in the name of Christ, if these things are not true; and if ye shall ask with a sincere heart, with real intent, having faith in Christ, he will manifest the truth of it unto you, by the power of the Holy Ghost. And by the power of the Holy Ghost ye may know the truth of all things.
(Moroni 10:4-5)

Visual Aid:
GAPK # 512
Heber J. Grant

Heber J. Grant's father died when he was thirteen days old, and he and his mother didn't have very much money. Heber said that when he was a boy, they had six dishes, and two of those were cracked.

Heber didn't live far from the prophet Brigham Young's home, though, and after school he would sometimes see Brigham pass by driving his sleigh.

One day, Heber jumped onto the back of Brigham's sleigh. He planned to hold on for a free ride and then jump off near his home. But soon the horses picked up speed. Not knowing what to do, Heber tightened his grip. Soon Brigham's sleigh was out of the city and flying through the countryside.

Heber was too scared to even yell. Then the sleigh slowed down to pass through a small stream, and Brigham saw Heber holding on for dear life.

Brigham pulled Heber into the sleigh and invited him to join his family for prayer each night. As Heber listened to those prayers, he began to feel closer to Heavenly Father, all because of a wild sleigh ride.[5]

A reading contest created a testimony

By the time Heber J. Grant was a deacon, he did his best to memorize important teachings of the Church. He could repeat every word of the Articles of Faith and the Word of Wisdom. However, Heber was very shy. When he was asked to speak in front of the whole Sunday School, he said he shook "like a leaf." But each time, he prayed for strength, and he would somehow make it through his talk.

Soon after, Heber's uncle Anthony Ivins invited Heber to have a reading contest with Anthony's son, who was Heber's cousin. His uncle said that the first boy to read the Book of Mormon all the way through would win a pair of nice gloves. Heber agreed, even though he wasn't a fast reader. Sure enough, his cousin jumped ahead by several pages.

Heber gave up hope of winning, but he kept reading the book anyway. When he finished, he discovered that after a fast start, his cousin had never finished the book. Heber said, " When I finished the book, I not only got a testimony of the gospel, but I got the gloves as well!" [6]

Scripture

O, remember, my son, and learn wisdom in thy youth; yea, learn in thy youth to keep the commandments of God. (Alma 37:35)

Visual Aid:
GAPK # 512
Heber J. Grant

David O. McKay obeyed the Word of Wisdom

Scripture:

He that hath my commandments, and keepeth them, he it is that loveth me: and he that loveth me shall be loved of my Father, and I will love him, and will manifest myself to him.
(John 14:21)

Visual Aid:
GAPK # 514
David O. McKay

President David O. McKay began his life as a farm boy in Huntsville, Utah, where his parents taught him the importance of obeying the Word of Wisdom. That commandment teaches us not to drink coffee, tea or beer, or to smoke cigarettes. President McKay promised himself that he would never do those things.

Many years later, he was invited to visit with the queen of the Netherlands, a country in Europe. They had a nice talk for several minutes, then a servant brought in a cup of tea for both of the them. The queen began drinking her tea, but then she saw that President McKay hadn't touched his cup.

The queen asked him about it, and President McKay told her that drinking tea was against his beliefs. The queen got a little angry. She said, "You won't even have a drink of tea with the queen of the Netherlands?"

President McKay said, "Would you ask me to do something that I teach the people of my church not to do?" The queen thought for a moment, then said, "I won't ask you to do that." She was impressed that he had honored his beliefs.[7]

George Albert Smith was a peacemaker

George Albert Smith grew up in a small house that didn't even have a lawn. But one summer George decided to do something about it. He saved up enough money to buy some grass seed, then after he planted it, he carried buckets of water from an irrigation ditch each night to water it. By the end of summer, the house had a beautiful lawn. This made George's family very happy.

When George was a young man, he had an accident that caused him to lose the sight in one eye. This was a hard thing for him, but it made him humble and taught him to be more helpful to those around him.

One way he tried to make others happy was by going to hospitals, playing his guitar and singing funny songs. This made the people laugh and forget their troubles for a little while. Beneath George's funny songs, though, was a strong desire to follow the Savior and be a peacemaker. Throughout his life, he did his best to make other people feel good about themselves.

After his death, people said George Albert Smith was "the kindest man who ever lived." We can follow his example and bring peace to our homes.[8]

Scripture

Blessed are the peacemakers: for they shall be called the children of God. (Matthew 5:9)

Visual Aid:
GAPK # 513
George Albert Smith

Chapter 5:

Family members have important responsibilities

Righteous fathers listen to the Holy Ghost

When Heavenly Father sent Jesus to earth, he made sure he had faithful parents who listened to the Holy Ghost. When Jesus was a small child, King Herod heard that a baby had been born who would become the King of the Jews. This made him angry and he told his soldiers to kill all the young babies. But the Lord warned Joseph to take Jesus and Mary to Egypt and save their lives. Joseph was a righteous man who protected Jesus.

Another righteous father who listened to the Holy Ghost was Wilford Woodruff. One time he was traveling in a wagon with his family. They stopped along the road and tied his wagon and horses under a big tree to sleep for the night. A few hours later, Wilford woke up in the middle of the night and moved his wagon. His wife asked him what he was doing. He said he didn't know, but that the Holy Ghost had told him to do it.

Twenty minutes later a tornado came that blew down the big tree. It landed right where the wagon had been. The Woodruff family would have been killed. Wilford was glad he had listened to the Holy Ghost.[9]

Helaman's young men obeyed their mothers

In the Book of Mormon there is a story about two thousand young Nephite warriors. They were led by a man named Helaman. The Nephites were being attacked by an army of wicked Lamanites, and many of the older Nephite soldiers had been killed. Helaman needed the young men to help protect their nation.

Helaman felt sad about asking these young men to fight in the war, but they told him they were willing to fight to protect their families. The young men told Helaman they had been taught by their mothers that if they would have faith and keep the commandments, Heavenly Father would watch over them.

The battle was fierce, but with the help of the young men, the Nephites were able to defend their nation. When the battle was over, all of the young men had been hurt. Some had lost so much blood that they fainted. But not one of them had died. The Nephites knew that Heavenly Father had blessed these young men because they had obeyed the teachings of their mothers.

If we listen to and obey the teachings of our own mothers, we will also be blessed.

Scripture

Now they never had fought, yet they did not fear death; and they did think more upon the liberty of their fathers than they did upon their lives; yea, they had been taught by their mothers, that if they did not doubt, God would deliver them. (Alma 56:47)

Visual Aid:
GAPK # 313
Two Thousand Young Warriors

Brigham Young believed his mother's words

When Brigham young was a child, his family lived on a farm in Vermont. Sometimes it was a hard life, especially when his mother became sick. She became very weak and wasn't able to do the chores that mothers usually do.

Brigham was asked by his father to help do these chores. So Brigham not only helped his father with the farm chores, such as chopping down trees and milking the cows, but also he also learned how to make bread, wash the dishes and make butter. Brigham learned the importance of hard work, and this helped him when he grew up and became a carpenter.

Brigham's mother knew she would die soon, so she did her best to teach him stories about Jesus from the Bible. She died when Brigham was fourteen, but her teachings made him into a righteous man. He always remembered the Bible stories she had taught him.[10]

Heavenly Father wants us to help our parents, especially when they aren't feeling well. If we honor our parents, our families will be blessed.

Emma Smith cared for Joseph's mother

When the Prophet Joseph Smith was killed by wicked men in Carthage Jail, it was a very hard time for his wife Emma. She had lost her husband and was left to care for several small children.

This was also a hard time for Joseph's mother Lucy. In a very short time her husband and three of her sons had died. She was feeling sad and alone.

Emma invited Lucy to live with her in Nauvoo, Illinois. These two great women had been through many difficulties together, and now they were able to help and strengthen each other during these hard times.

Lucy never lost her faith in Heavenly Father. Since she was too old and weak to travel across the plains to Salt Lake City with the rest of the members of the Church, she stayed in Nauvoo. She was a happy person and had fun with her grandchildren. She also made sure she taught them about the Savior and the important works their father Joseph had done.[11]

Heavenly Father is happy when we show love and respect to our grandparents and other family members.

Scripture

Hear, ye children, the instruction of a father, and attend to know understanding.
(Proverbs 4:1)

Visual Aid:
GAPK # 405
Emma Smith

Chapter 6:

Heavenly Father teaches me how to strengthen my family

The Savior taught about family prayer

After the Savior's resurrection, he visited the people who were living in the Americas. These people first heard the Savior's voice coming from heaven, then they watched him come down from the sky.

Jesus then taught the people about the gospel. One of the first things he taught them was about prayer. He said it was very important to say our prayers to Heavenly Father.

Saying a prayer is like talking to Heavenly Father. We can thank him for what he has given us, and we can also ask him for the things we need.

Jesus said we should each pray on our own, but that we should also pray together as families. He said that when we pray, it helps protect us from the evil things of the world. It also helps us remember to keep Heavenly Father's commandments.

Our modern prophets have given to us the same message. They have promised us that if we say our prayers together as families, Heavenly Father will bless all the members of our family.

Scripture:

Pray in your families unto the Father, always in my name, that your wives and your children may be blessed.
(3 Nephi 18:21)

Visual Aid:
GAPK # 316
Jesus Teaching in the Western Hemisphere

Lehi knew the value of the scriptures

The scriptures are the most important books in the world. They are filled with important messages from Heavenly Father.

The prophet Lehi knew how important the scriptures are. When he left Jerusalem with his family, they traveled for three days in the desert. Then Lehi realized that they had forgotten their scriptures, which were written on the brass plates.

Lehi knew that his family needed to have the brass plates before they traveled to the Promised Land. Lehi knew that without the brass plates, his family would soon forget many important parts of the gospel.

So Lehi sent his sons back to get the brass plates, even though it would take them three days traveling across the desert to return to Jerusalem. He knew Heavenly Father wanted them to have the scriptures.

We are blessed to have the scriptures in our homes. The prophet has asked us to read our scriptures each day as a family. Heavenly Father will bless us if we read the scriptures together and live their teachings.

Scripture

And upon these I write the things of my soul, and many of the scriptures which are engraven upon the plates of brass. For my soul delighteth in the scriptures, and my heart pondereth them, and writeth them for the learning and the profit of my children.
(2 Nephi 4:15)

Visual Aid:
GAPK # 304
Lehi and His People Arrive in the Promised Land

John Taylor still had a bullet in his leg

Scripture:

Therefore, go ye unto your homes, and ponder upon the things which I have said, and ask of the Father, in my name, that ye may understand, and prepare your minds for the morrow, and I come unto you again.
(3 Nephi 17:3)

Visual Aid:
GAPK # 508
John Taylor

John Taylor was a busy man, but he did his best to make his family the most important thing in his life. He tried to gather his children around him each night for family prayer and to share his testimony. John Taylor would tell them about when he was in Carthage Jail on the day Joseph Smith was killed. Several bullets fired by the mob also hit John Taylor, but he somehow survived.

Many years later, he would tell his children about that day, and he would let them feel a bullet that was still stuck under the skin of his left leg.

John Taylor enjoyed playing checkers and other simple games with his children. He also made sure they were reading good books. One time his son won a new novel called *Twenty Thousand Leagues Under the Sea* as a prize at school. To make sure the book was good material for his son, John Taylor stayed up all night reading it. In the morning he said, "That's a good book, son. You may read it."[12]

Like John Taylor, we can help our family choose good entertainment and keep the Holy Ghost with us.

Joseph couldn't translate after an argument

Joseph Smith loved all people, and especially little children. He always did his best to say a kind word and shake hands with any little children he saw. He tried to make everyone around him feel happy.

However, one day Joseph felt a little grumpy. He had been upstairs in his house translating the gold plates, but then he took a break. He went downstairs, and ended up in a small argument with his wife Emma.

When Joseph went back upstairs to translate again, he couldn't do it. He wondered what was wrong, and then he realized his argument with Emma had made him lose the spirit of the Lord.

Joseph went back downstairs and apologized to Emma. He told her he was sorry they had argued. They gave each other a small hug and then he went back upstairs. This time he was able to translate again.

Joseph had learned that when we are angry, it is hard to feel the Holy Ghost in our lives. We can strengthen our family by being kind and keeping a peaceful spirit in our home.[13]

Scripture

And he commanded them that there should be no contention one with another, but that they should look forward with one eye, having one faith and one baptism, having their hearts knit together in unity and in love one towards another.
(Mosiah 18:21)

Visual Aid:
GAPK # 420
The Prophet Joseph
Loved Children

Chapter 7:

Temples unite families

Harold B. Lee shared his musical talents

Scripture:

And whoso believeth in me, and is baptized, the same shall be saved; and they are they who shall inherit the kingdom of God.
(3 Nephi 11:33)

Visual Aid:
GAPK # 516
Harold B. Lee

When Harold B. Lee was growing up, he really didn't like practicing the piano. But he kept practicing, and by the time he went on his mission, he played very well.

During his mission, Harold was in a city where nobody wanted to listen to the gospel message. Then Harold received a new missionary companion, Elder Willis Woodbury, who had a good idea about how to get people to listen to them.

Elder Woodbury played an instrument called the cello (*chell-o*), which is like a big violin. When they went out to knock on doors, Elder Woodbury would carry his scriptures in one hand, and the cello case in the other. If the missionaries saw a piano in a home, they would ask the people if they could play some music for them.

Suddenly many more people wanted to listen to their message. Several of these people were baptized into the Church and later were sealed as families in the temple.

Harold later would play the piano during meetings of the Quorum of the Twelve Apostles in the Salt Lake Temple. We can bless others through our talents.[14]

Spencer Kimball wanted to be worthy

When Spencer W. Kimball's mission ended, he began going to college at the University of Arizona. He worked very hard to get good grades, and he would study all Saturday night. But one Sunday he didn't wake up in time to make it to Church.

Then the next Sunday he found himself sleeping in again. He looked at the clock and knew he could still make it to his church meetings if he got ready quickly.

Spencer closed his eyes to go to sleep again, but then he jumped out of bed and looked in the mirror. He said outloud, "What are you doing, Spencer Kimball? This is the way that people fall away from the Church."

He went to church that week, and every week after that. Spencer had received a strong feeling he would soon meet his future wife, and he wanted to be worthy to marry her in the temple.

Within a few months he met Camilla Eyring, and they fell in love. They were soon sealed in the temple.[15]

We should follow President Kimball's example and help our family be worthy to attend the temple.

Scripture

For behold, this life is the time for men to prepare to meet God; yea, behold the day of this life is the day for men to perform their labors.
(Alma 34:32)

Visual Aid:
GAPK # 517
Spencer W. Kimball

Elijah has restored the sealing power

Scripture:

The Prophet Elijah was to plant in the hearts of the children the promises made to their fathers; Foreshadowing the great work to be done in the temples of the Lord in the dispensation of the fulness of times, for the redemption of the dead, and the sealing of the children to their parents, lest the whole earth be smitten with a curse and utterly wasted at his coming.
(D&C 138:47-48)

Visual Aid:
GAPK # 417
Elijah Restores the Power to
Seal Families for Eternity

Elijah was a prophet that lived in Israel many years before the birth of Jesus. He loved Heavenly Father very much, and was righteous in all that he did. Heavenly Father was happy with him and gave him the sealing power, meaning that whatever Elijah wanted would be approved by Heavenly Father.

After many years, this power was lost because of the wickedness of the people. But in the Bible is a prophecy that says Elijah would return in the latter days and restore the sealing power to the earth.

That prophecy was fulfilled on April 3, 1836, when Elijah returned to earth as a resurrected person. On that day Elijah visited Joseph Smith in the Kirtland Temple. He gave Joseph the keys to this sealing power, which includes sealing families together in eternal marriage. Ever since Elijah came, people all over the world have become very interested in family history work and temple work.

We can be sealed together as families through the covenants and ordinances of the temple.

The Nauvoo Saints wanted temple blessings

Soon after the prophet Joseph Smith was killed, the members of the Church felt they should move to the Rocky Mountains. But they didn't want to leave until the Nauvoo Temple was finished, so they could receive their temple blessings.

By early 1846, the temple was finished enough that temple ordinances could be performed. Brigham Young wanted as many of the people as possible to attend the temple before they had to move. He knew that this would give them spiritual power as they began their trip across the plains to their new home.

For many days, Brigham and other men who held the priesthood spent all day and night in the temple helping hundreds of other members receive their temple blessings, because they knew they wouldn't have another temple for many years.[16]

Brigham Young knew the importance of temple work, and we can follow his example by doing family history work for our ancestors. This helps us unite our family so we can live together forever someday.

Scripture

Behold, I will send you Elijah the prophet before the coming of the great and dreadful day of the Lord: And he shall turn the heart of the fathers to the children, and the heart of the children to their fathers, lest I come and smite the earth with a curse.
(Malachi 4:5-6)

Visual Aid:
GAPK # 410
Exodus from Nauvoo,
Feb.-May 1846

Chapter 8:

Faith, prayer, repentance, and forgiveness can strengthen my family

Harold B. Lee safely guided his daughters

Scripture:

Look unto me in every thought; doubt not, fear not.
(D&C 6:36)

When Harold B. Lee's daughters were young, he took the family to visit Timpanogos Cave in the mountains a few miles south of Salt Lake City.

Sister Lee wasn't feeling too well, so she decided not to make the steep hike to the cave, but she warned her daughters to stay away from the edge of the trail, and to not let go of their father's hand.

One of her daughters said, "Mommy, you don't have to worry about us. As long as Daddy's here, we'll be just fine. We'll be safe."

The girls trusted their father as they walked along the narrow trail with its steep dropoffs. As they reached the cave opening, Harold told his daughters he was glad that they trusted him, but that there was someone else that they should trust even more—Heavenly Father.

Harold told them that whatever dangers they faced in their lives, they could always call upon Heavenly Father to help them fight temptations.

If we have faith in Heavenly Father, he will help us stay away from all kinds of dangers.[17]

Visual Aid:
GAPK # 516
Harold B. Lee

Misbehaving boys were told to walk

David O. McKay was a kind father who wanted his children to live righteously.

One day, President McKay and his family were driving home after a long trip, but his two sons in the back seat were acting badly. They were yelling loudly and hitting each other. President McKay told them they needed to stop fighting, but they didn't listen to him.

Finally when they were about two miles from home, President McKay stopped the car at the bottom of a big hill and calmly told his boys to get out the car. He told them that because they had kept fighting, they could walk the rest of the way home.

The boys were very surprised, but they also knew they hadn't obeyed their father. So they got out of the car and watched the car disappear over the hill.

The boys walked up the steep hill and were very happy to see the family car waiting at the top. The boys climbed back into the car and told their father they were sorry. They were quiet all the way home and had learned an important lesson about obeying their parents.[18]

Scripture

And they shall also teach their children to pray, and to walk uprightly before the Lord.
(D&C 68:28)

Visual Aid:
GAPK # 514
David O. McKay

Alma the Younger chose to repent of his sins

Alma the Younger was the prophet's son, but he chose to live a wicked life. He even tried to destroy the Church and teach the people to do wicked things.

This made his father very sad. But his father prayed that Heavenly Father would help Alma change his life and do what is right.

One day when Alma was on his way to do more wicked things, an angel appeared to him. The angel's voice sounded like thunder, because he was very angry with how Alma had been living his life. The angel told Alma that if he didn't repent he would never live in heaven.

Alma was so frightened by the angel's words that he fainted and wouldn't wake up. He stayed asleep for two days. While he was asleep, the Lord showed Alma all the wicked things he had done. Alma saw that the only way to heaven was to follow the Savior.

Alma woke up and told everyone he had been wrong. He repented of his sins and taught the people about the gospel of Jesus Christ for the rest of his life.

To be forgiven, we must forgive others

The prophets have taught us the importance of forgiving others if they have hurt us.

When Spencer W. Kimball was an apostle he was asked to visit a ward where the members had let a little argument between two people turn into a big fight that had divided the ward. Many people had stopped going to church, and President Kimball was very worried.

President Kimball arrived at the church and listened to the people argue. This went on for several hours. Finally President Kimball told everyone to be quiet. Then he gave a powerful talk about forgiveness.

He told them to think of the Savior, and how people had treated him badly, but that the Savior had forgiven the people who had hurt him. President Kimball said that we should be like the Savior and forgive others. Then Heavenly Father would forgive our sins.

The ward members listened to President Kimball. They knew they had acted badly and needed to forgive each other. The people told each other they were sorry, and the people became friends once again.[19]

Scripture

Wherefore, I say unto you, that ye ought to forgive one another; for he that forgiveth not his brother his trespasses standeth condemned before the Lord; for there remaineth in him the greater sin. I, the Lord, will forgive whom I will forgive, but of you it is required to forgive all men.
(D&C 64:9-10)

Visual Aid:
GAPK # 517
Spencer W. Kimball

Chapter 9: Respect, love, work, and wholesome recreation can strengthen my family

Scripture:

Therefore all things what-soever ye would that men should do to you, do ye even so to them: for this is the law and the prophets. (Matthew 7:12)

Visual Aid:
GAPK # 515
Joseph Fielding Smith

Joseph Fielding Smith loved his family very much. When he was working in his office, he would leave his office door open and told his secretary that if she saw any of his family members pass by, she should invite them in to see him.

President Smith had to make many trips across the world as an apostle, but he always kept his family in mind. When he was gone on these trips, he would wear two watches—one on each wrist. He would have one set on the time at home in Salt Lake City and the other one set on the time where he was. That way he could think about what his family was doing at that moment, no matter where he was in the world.

He learned his great love for his family from his father, President Joseph F. Smith. He greatly respected his father, and at times when he was tempted, he would ask himself, "What would my father think of that?"

This reminded him that Heavenly Father was also watching him. We can follow President Smith's example and show love and respect to our own families.[20]

The Kimball family trusted in the Lord

Before Spencer W. Kimball became an apostle, he worked selling land and insurance in Arizona, but the year 1933 was a very hard year across the world. It was called the Great Depression, because very few people had jobs. Spencer's company wasn't doing very well, and they didn't have much money, but Spencer and his wife Camilla trusted that Heavenly Father would help them if they stayed faithful to the gospel.

Then the Kimballs' three-year-old son Eddie got very sick with a disease called polio. The doctor in Arizona thought Eddie was going to die, so Camilla took him to a special doctor in California. Spencer stayed in Arizona with their three other children. It was a time that could have made their family grow apart. But the family wrote many letters back and forth, and everyone realized how much they meant to each other.

Eddie lived through the disease, but for many years his legs were very weak. The whole family helped him return to normal strength. The Kimballs learned that life isn't always easy, but that the Lord will be with us.[21]

Scripture

A new commandment I give unto you, That ye love one another; as I have loved you, that ye also love one another. By this shall all men know that ye are my disciples, if ye have love one to another.
(John 13:34-35)

Visual Aid:
GAPK # 517
Spencer W. Kimball

Six days shalt thou labour, and do all thy work. (Exodus 20:9)

When David O. McKay was six years old, his family went through a very hard time. One of his sisters died from an illness, and then on the morning of her funeral, another sister died. The two sisters were buried in the same grave.

This was a sad time for David, but he knew that his sisters had returned to live with Heavenly Father.

A few months later, David's father was called to serve a mission in Scotland, thousands of miles away. So little David and his mother took care of the farm.

The family had planned to add on a room to their home, but it looked like that project would have to wait unto David's father returned home. But David's mother wanted to surprise her husband.

With the help of some neighbors, David and his mother built the new room. They kept it a secret from David's father, and he was very surprised and happy to return from his mission to find the room already built.[22]

Working together, especially in hard times, can help strengthen and build love in our families.

Even the prophets take time to have fun

One of the best ways for families to grow closer is by playing games and fun activities together. This will help develop unity and love for each other.

Brigham Young's family worked hard together as they helped build Salt Lake City, but they also enjoyed games that helped relax their minds and bodies.

Brigham really liked to attend the theatre. Many of his children were in the plays, and he was there almost every night that he didn't have a church meeting.

The church members in Brigham's time also liked to hold family dances, where everyone could come, no matter how old they were. Brigham himself was a good dancer, and one person said Brigham would dance "with glee and zest," meaning he really had a fun time.[23]

One way that Wilford Woodruff liked to relax was to go fishing in mountain streams. If he went to visit church members, he would take along his fishing pole, just in case he saw a good fishing hole along the way.[24]

We can follow the example of the prophets and take time to relax and have fun with our families.

Scripture

And ye will not have a mind to injure one another, but to live peaceably, and to render to every man according to that which is his due.
(Mosiah 4:13)

Visual Aid:
GAPK # 509
Wilford Woodruff

Chapter 10:

Prophets teach me how to strengthen my family

Joseph of Egypt treated his brothers well

Scripture:

Honour thy father and thy mother: that thy days may be long upon the land which the Lord thy God giveth thee.
(Exodus 20:12)

Visual Aid:
GAPK # 109
Joseph Is Sold By His Brothers

The prophet Jacob had twelve sons. One son named Joseph was very righteous. He obeyed his father.

But Joseph's brothers weren't happy with Joseph. They didn't like the attention he received from Jacob for being good, so one day they sold him to be a slave. The brothers hoped they would never see Joseph again.

Joseph was taken to Egypt. At first, he was a slave, but because of his faithfulness, he helped the king of Egypt and became a leader, too.

A few years later, it didn't rain for a long time. The crops wouldn't grow, and the people were starving. Jacob sent his sons to ask the king of Egypt for food. They were met by Joseph, who recognized his brothers, but they didn't know it was him.

He teased them a little, but then he gave them the food they needed. He told them who he was and asked them to bring their father Jacob to live with him. He honored his father, and he treated his brothers well, despite how they had treated him. Joseph is a great example of how we should treat our family members.

King Benjamin taught by example

Many of the kings in the Book of Mormon didn't follow Heavenly Father's teachings. These kings would make their people work very hard so that they could have fancy clothes and live in big houses. Heavenly Father would send prophets to teach the people, but these wicked kings would kill them.

Then came along a king who was different. His name was King Benjamin. Rather than killing the prophets, we was happy to have his people learn the gospel.

The Book of Mormon says that King Benjamin was a holy man, meaning he liked to do what was right. Many people were surprised that King Benjamin didn't want to be rich. He just wanted to be a righteous person and help other people.

King Benjamin taught his people that giving service to each other was a way of helping Heavenly Father. Soon, all the people in his kingdom wanted to be like him. He is a great example to us, too. If we give service to others, Heavenly Father will bless us and we'll feel good inside for doing what is right.

Scripture

But ye will teach them to walk in the ways of truth and soberness; ye will teach them to love one another, and to serve one another.
(Mosiah 4:15)

Visual Aid:
GAPK # 307
King Benjamin
Addresses His People

The Bensons read it in the newspaper

Scripture:

If ye love me, keep my commandments.
(John 14:15)

In 1915, President Joseph F. Smith announced the Family Home Evening program, but this was before radio and TV had been invented. So many of the church members didn't find out about the new program for a long time.

Ezra Taft Benson was a young man at that time. His family lived on a farm in Idaho. One day his father was reading the newspaper before dinner. Then he jumped up and told them to listen closely. He read to the family a story in the newspaper that said the prophet had started a new program for families to meet together one night each week.

Ezra's father said they were going to follow the prophet's teachings. They really didn't know what to do, but they started holding Family Home Evening that very night. They sang songs and read from the scriptures.

Ezra remembered one of those early lessons for the rest of his life. He said, "One lesson my father taught me was that Heavenly Father is always near." If we hold Family Home Evening, our family will be blessed.[25]

Visual Aid:
GAPK # 518
Ezra Taft Benson

President Hinckley teaches us the right way

The prophet today teaches us how to strengthen our families. President Gordon B. Hinckley and his wife Sister Marjorie Hinckley raised five children.

They said it wasn't always easy, but Sister Hinckley said having laughter and fun in their home was important. She said, "If we can't laugh at life, we are in big trouble."

President and Sister Hinckley hope that every child in the church enjoys Primary and won't miss a week. They know Primary helps us grow closer to Heavenly Father.

Sister Hinckley said, "One of our daughters decided to stay home from church one Sunday. So she stayed home. She got very lonely. Everybody was in church but her, and she just sat on the lawn. She didn't try that again."

We should be grateful that we have a living prophet and his faithful wife to guide us and share what he has learned during his life. President and Sister Hinckley love us and want us to live righteous, happy lives.[26]

Scripture

And the King shall answer and say unto them, Verily I say unto you, Inasmuch as ye have done it unto one of the least of these my brethren, ye have done it unto me.
(Matthew 25:40)

Visual Aid:
GAPK # 520
Gordon B. Hinckley

Chapter 11:

Keeping the Sabbath day holy can strengthen my family

Harold B. Lee hated his long, curly hair

And that thou mayest more fully keep thyself unspotted from the world, thou shalt go to the house of prayer and offer up thy sacraments upon my holy day.
(D&C 59:9)

Visual Aid:
GAPK # 516
Harold B. Lee

When Harold B. Lee was five years old, he hated going to Primary because he had long hair. His mother loved how his hair curled, and she let to grow almost to his shoulders. But the other children, including his brothers, often made fun of him.

Their teasing words made Harold sad, so one day he cut off as much of his hair as he could. But he didn't use a mirror, and it was really short in some places and still long in others. His mother started crying when she saw his head, but his brothers were glad. They helped Harold shave off the rest of his hair. So now, with very short hair, Harold liked going to Primary.

As he grew older, he loved Sunday and the good feelings he had at Church. He knew it was a special day, and he promised not to go swimming in their pond on Sunday. Instead, his family spent the day singing and enjoying each other's company. And the best part, Harold said, was he didn't have to do chores! He knew Sunday is a day to remember Heavenly Father.[27]

There are many fun things to do on Sunday

Sometimes it might feel like the prophets say that we can't do anything on Sunday except go to Church. That is not true. There are many fun things we can do with our families on Sunday.

The prophets have asked us to do activities that we might not have time to do during the rest of the week. President Kimball gave a list of things that we can do that will help us keep the Sabbath day holy.

He said we could read the scriptures and Church magazines, like *The Friend*. We can also study the lives and teachings of the prophets.

President Kimball said some families write in their journals or work on family history on that day. It is also a good day to visit relatives and friends, write letters to missionaries, and sing Church hymns.

President Kimball also said we can use Sunday to plan the upcoming Family Night lesson.[28]

As we keep the Sabbath day holy, our families will be blessed and the Holy Ghost will be with us.

Scripture

For verily this is a day appointed unto you to rest from your labors, and to pay thy devotions unto the Most High.
(D&C 59:10)

Visual Aid:
GAPK # 617
Search the Scriptures

Joseph Fielding Smith learned a great lesson

Scripture:

Yea, and are willing to mourn with those that mourn; yea, and comfort those that stand in need of comfort, and to stand as witnesses of God at all times and in all things, and in all places that ye may be in, even until death, that ye may be redeemed of God, and be numbered with those of the first resurrection, that ye may have eternal life.
(Mosiah 18:9)

Visual Aid:
GAPK # 515
Joseph Fielding Smith

When Joseph Fielding Smith was called to serve a mission in England, he was very excited. He knew that many of the early members of the church had come from England. But when he served his mission, nearly everyone in England was poor. Nobody wanted to be baptized into the church, partly because they didn't want to pay tithing. The people told the missionaries they didn't have enough money to do that.

So when Joseph finished his mission, he felt a little sorry for himself. He had taught many people, but he didn't baptize anyone during his whole time in England!

When Joseph came home, he heard his friends talk about the people they had baptized. It almost made him want to cry. But Joseph's father knew what was most important. He told Joseph that he was proud of him, and that he had served a good mission. He had done his best and had learned the importance of working hard.

Most important of all, he had served his Heavenly Father. The lessons Joseph learned on his mission helped him become a great man.[29]

Fasting can bring blessings from heaven

In our church we sometimes talk about fasting. Fasting means to not eat or drink for many hours as a way to grow closer to Heavenly Father. It helps our spirit be in tune with the Holy Ghost, but President Joseph F. Smith taught that the church members need to be wise when fasting.

President Smith said some people might be weak or too sick to fast. He taught that such people "should not be required to fast." He also taught that parents should not make their little children fast.

He said, "I have known children to cry for something to eat on fast day. In such cases, going without food will do them no good. Better to teach them the principle, and let them observe it when they are old enough to choose."

President Smith then said, "But those should fast who can. It is required of the Saints in every part of the Church." [30]

As we grow older, we can choose to fast and bring blessings to our families.

Scripture

Nevertheless they did fast and pray oft, and did wax stronger and stronger in their humility, and firmer and firmer in the faith of Christ, unto the filling their souls with joy and consolation.
(Helaman 3:35)

Visual Aid:
GAPK # 511
Joseph F. Smith

Chapter 12:

My family is blessed when we remember Jesus Christ

The Sacrament reminds us of the Savior

Scripture:

And as they were eating, Jesus took bread, and blessed it, and brake it, and gave it to the disciples, and said, Take, eat; this is my body. And he took the cup, and gave thanks, and gave it to them, saying, Drink ye all of it; For this is my blood of the new testament, which is shed for many for the remission of sins.
(Matthew 26:26-28)

Visual Aid:
GAPK # 225
The Last Supper

An important way our family can live the gospel is to attend our church meetings each Sunday and take the Sacrament.

During the last week of his life, Jesus told his apostles about the Sacrament. He taught that the bread represents his body, and the water is a reminder that he bled and suffered to take away our sins.

When Joseph Smith restored the Church to the earth in 1830, the Sacrament was the first ordinance that he performed.

We still take the Sacrament each week to remind us of the sacrifice Jesus made for us. This is a time for us to be very reverent and to think about all the wonderful things the Savior has done for us.

We need to always remember that Jesus paid the price for our sins, and if we repent we can return to live in heaven.

If we try to do what is right every day, and then take the Sacrament each week, we are doing what Heavenly Father has asked us to do.

Jesus was born into a special family

Heavenly Father planned for Jesus to be born into a family that would love and protect him as he grew up. Mary was a wonderful mother who came from a special family. Many of her ancestors were great heroes in the Bible.

The prophets Abraham, Isaac and Jacob were in her family line, as well as Ruth, a great example of faith.

Another of her ancestors was David, the young boy who killed the giant Goliath.

But as important as these ancestors were, the most important thing that the Savior's earthly parents did was teach Jesus about Heavenly Father and raised him in a righteous family.

We are also part of a special family. When we are baptized into The Church of Jesus Christ of Latter-day Saints, we are on our way to returning to live with our Heavenly Father again.

If we keep the commandments and follow the Savior's example, we will find happiness in this life, and then be welcomed back into our heavenly home.

Scripture

So all the generations from Abraham to David are fourteen generations; and from David until the carrying away into Babylon are fourteen generations; and from the carrying away into Babylon unto Christ are fourteen generations.
(Matthew 1:17)

Visual Aid:
GAPK # 242
Jesus And His Mother

Scripture:

And behold, I tell you these things that ye may learn wisdom; that ye may learn that when ye are in the service of your fellow beings ye are only in the service of your God. (Mosiah 2:17)

The Savior loves us very much. He has paid the price for our sins. We can show how grateful we are for what he has done by doing good deeds for other people.

When David O. McKay was a young boy, he gave service to the church by cutting wood for the chapel's fireplaces. This would take several hours to cut the wood and then stack it by the fireplaces, but David felt good inside knowing that the ward members would be warm during their Sunday meetings.[31] We now have nice church buildings with furnaces, but there are other ways we can give service.

Some Primary groups help keep the church grounds clean by picking up litter and pulling weeds. We should all look around our seats after Sacrament Meeting to and make sure we've picked up everything we brought, such as papers or snacks.

One of the greatest gifts we can give to the Savior is to be kind to others and set a good example. He is very happy when we show reverence at church and act kindly toward our family members and friends.

Visual Aid:
GAPK # 514
David O. McKay

The Savior will soon come again

The day is soon coming when Jesus Christ will return to earth again. This is called the Second Coming. Jesus will come in the sky, with many angels at his side. At that time, the earth will be cleansed. The righteous will be protected, and the wicked will be burned by fire. Then the Savior will live on earth again, and there will be one thousand years of peace.

The members of the Church are helping prepare for that time. Missionaries are teaching the gospel to people all over the world, telling them about the Savior and helping them be ready for the Second Coming.

The Savior wants us to be ready for that day, too. He has told his prophets that one of the most important things we can do is help our family members live righteously. We should all have the goal to be worthy to attend the temple.

Some of the things that we can do is have family prayer, read scriptures together, and attend our meetings each Sunday. If we keep the commandments, we will be happy when Jesus comes again.

Scripture

For the Son of man shall come in the glory of his Father with his angels; and then he shall reward every man according to his works.
(Matthew 16:27)

Visual Aid:
GAPK # 239
The Resurrected Jesus Christ

References

1. Arrington, Leonard J., editor. *The Presidents of the Church*, Deseret Book, 1986, p. 137.

2. Ibid., p. 162.

3. Ibid., p. 57-58.

4. Kimball, Edward L., and Andrew E. Kimball, Jr. *Spencer W. Kimball*. Salt Lake City, Utah: Bookcraft, 1977, p. 33.

5.Arrington, Leonard J., editor. *The Presidents of the Church*, Deseret Book, 1986, p. 217-218.

6. Ibid., p. 222-224.

7. Ibid., p. 303-304.

8. Ibid., p. 252-253, 271.

9. Ibid., p. 129.

10. Ibid., p. 44-45.

11. Ludlow, Daniel H., editor. *Encyclopedia of Mormonism*. New York: Macmillan Publishing Company, 1992, p. 1357.

12. Arrington, Leonard J., editor. *The Presidents of the Church*, edited by Leonard J. Arrington, Deseret Book, 1986, p. 101.

13. Ibid., p. 17.

14. Ibid., p. 352, 363.

15. Ibid., p. 377-379.

16. Barrett, Ivan J. *Joseph Smith and the Restoration*, Brigham Young University Press, 1973, p. 635.

17. Arrington, Leonard J., editor. *The Presidents of the Church*, edited by Leonard J. Arrington, Deseret Book, 1986, p. 354-355.

18. Ibid., p. 292.

19. Ibid., p. 393.

20. Ibid., p. 336-337.

21. Ibid., p. 383.

22. Ibid., p. 277-278.

23. Ibid., p. 64-66.

24. Ibid., p. 134.

25. Ibid., p. 424.

26. *Ensign*, Oct. 2003, p. 22-27.

27.Arrington, Leonard J., editor. *The Presidents of the Church*, edited by Leonard J. Arrington, Deseret Book, 1986, p. 348-349.

28. *Ensign*, Jan. 1982, p. 3.

29.Arrington, Leonard J., editor. *The Presidents of the Church*, edited by Leonard J. Arrington, Deseret Book, 1986, p. 321-322.

30. Smith, Joseph F. *Gospel Doctrine*. Salt Lake City: Deseret Book, 1939, p. 244.

31.Arrington, Leonard J., editor. *The Presidents of the Church*, edited by Leonard J. Arrington, Deseret Book, 1986, p. 280.

Other volumes in the
Tiny Talks series:

Volume 1:
The Temple

Volume 2:
The Savior

Volume 3:
The Church of
Jesus Christ

About the authors

Photo courtesy of Jack Daybell

Tammy and Chad Daybell live in Springville, Utah, with their five children, a rabbit, a guinea pig, a turtle, and several fish.

Tammy Douglas Daybell loves her family, but doesn't like doing the dishes. She is very grateful she married someone who will do them for her. She enjoys reading, gardening, and playing on the swings at a neighborhood schoolyard with her children. She recently house-trained their rabbit. She is currently serving as the Cubmaster in their ward. In her spare time she is the webmaster for www.cdaybell.com.

Chad Daybell wrote his first novel, *The Murder of Dr. Jay and His Assistant*, in fourth grade. Only one copy was printed, but it was put in the school library so his friends could check it out. Chad now has that copy.

Chad passed his love of music to his children and they all enjoy dancing in the living room together. He also enjoys reading and playing catch with his sons.

In 1992 he graduated from BYU with a bachelor's degree in journalism, where he served as the City Editor of *The Daily Universe*. Later, he worked as a newspaper editor at *The Standard-Examiner* in Ogden, Utah. He currently is employed as the Managing Editor for Cedar Fort, Inc.

About the illustrator

Rhett E. Murray received a bachelor's degree from Southern Utah University in Fine Art, and a master's degree from Southern Utah University in Art Education. He also completed a bachelor's degree in